AF244135

Hills of Age

Hills of Age

Dick Sullivan

Coracle Books

By the same author:
Non fiction
Navvyman
The Nature of Things: Plato Now & Then

Some of the verses in this collection first appeared
in *Capperbar*, 2011 (first published as *Nostos 1–7*,
1998/9. Second edition, revised and re-titled
Capperbar, 2003. Third edition, with Preface, 2010.)

© Dick Sullivan 2018
ISBN 0 906280 19 2 = 978 0 906280 19 5

For Mary

Contents

1. Alien at Ease

Preface
Strong Arm Jack's on Rannoch Moor:
He needs new bluchers and a pedicure.

Moleskin Joe's on a mountainside
Unaware of God or Eastertide:

We're on the edge of Christendom
With a leaky old harmonium.

Return, 1988
And then the scent of beck at last
And coffee from the lilac flask.
Here rock is wrapped in river,
River plays with light.
Note it in despite
Of pity for your plight.

Brown-pooled, rock-floored,
Jam-jarred you could fish
For fish too little for a dish.

Eel trap's gone, I see, but
No one ever caught and elver
That I remember: a timber hut
It was in which to climb
Scented by clean river slime.

In the dug-out, Cumberland Ike
Takes his ease with a cutty pipe
Under a dam with a copper core:
Mardale's marred forever more.

Around here lurks
The Corporation Water Works:
The '30s linger on
In all you look upon.

Millennium on its axletree?
Here is 1943:
Boys with brylcreem'd hair
Em-bus for the picture house
And beer, while Errol Flynn
Has yet the war to win.

Here's the beginning of it all:
Trout-ringed, rain-ringed river,
Midge-itch and cuckoo call.

Mardale, 1943
A wartime boy
Could always hide
In that big box eel trap
(Slippery as an elver
In the dappled dark)
As war and a river
Rippled by outside.

Lancashire, 1944
A steam train stops
With acorn-corded blinds,
And window straps,
Like shaving strops.

A soldier, in war-worn battle dress,
Shackled under close arrest,
Offers chocolate to a child.

Liverpool, 1945
Who stood blind in that blackout city
With no way back to beck, fell or falls?

Country Cottage, 1955

Write a threnody
For what has ceased to be:
That altered look
Of country under snow,
Spinney and silt-grey brook
Flowing now so long ago.
Thanksgiving time when
Holly's rimmed with rime
And all is pale with mist
And frost. Dew condenses
Barbed as ice on fences,
Bristling on a rail,
Bucket-shaped in pail.

Under foot's the creak of snow.
Black mid-winter's bright
With snowlight in the night.
Lying on a flock-filled bed
You wait to live before you're dead.

And yet you were medusa'd into stone
By a letter in a letter box,
Or the ringing of a telephone.

Hell, we think, is only this –
A raging mind in its own abyss
While outside in summer shines the sun.

Northants, 1955

I'm sheltering under an oak
On a long deserted lane
Silent save for falling rain
And a cuckoo calling,
In the green humidity,
Of that day:

Then the shimmering
Of lane and oak and rain,
A sense of sadness
And of rest although
I do not yet connect
Eternity to beauty
And the intellect
Though there always came
That gift of grace
When summer lined the lane
With Queen Anne's Lace.

Aldershot, 1956

Five Battalion read the signs
By the gorge of Company Lines.
Stiff as ice we stood, rigid as a rock,
In the chasm of the barrack block.
A conscript army, we,
In barracks abandoned by the cavalry:
Victorian troopers canter by
To imperial outposts, there to die.

Colchester, 1957

In that army town the Bamboo
Coffee Bar has long closed down
And now, in age, the coffee shop
Is all the rage.

We had the comfort then of time.
Time surrounded us like day, or sound,
But night in silence now is rolling round.
Imperial city dark with coal
Your marching armies now grow old.

To the Cape

And then I was on my way
From Windhoek to Three Anchor Bay
Down by the Cape with little hope.

White, Malay, and Hottentot
In the melting pot of Rehoboth
Sixty years ago. Dust as grey as tow:
Grey grainless dust that clung.
I, outlander of outlandish tongue.

* * *

Sunday, and a wind pump
Screaked. Early heat.
Sweat that leaked
In runnels on a dusty face.

A streetless place of haphazard
Shacks. No one turned their
Backs. I was a man of glass
Less visible than the air
Through which I passed.
A girl without a chest
And no attempt
To hide contempt
Slid me a dish, dry as dust,
Of boerewors and drier bread.

* * *

Gumboots on a beach:
Each pace was a ripping up
Of roots. A dry white sun
Seemed to spin dust from air
As I stood by the roadside there.

A car trailed dust,
Twin vortices, to trickle
On the trees, drooping,
Waxy, dry. Day drooped
By by the dirt highway.

A truck, dust blasted
Free of rust, pulled up.
Leaning sideways in the back
Was a ramshackle stack
Of beds and tables, chairs
And chests of drawers.

Kalkrand. Silence from its hub
Spread in a circle wide around
The flattest and most soundless ground.
Railroad track and shacks.
Earth was a hammered disc
Where to run was to run the risk
Of spinning all untethered off.

A loco way out there
Dipped and curtsied in oil-like air
Swelling and shrinking to the beat
Of haze and heat. "Such black smoke,"
Some one spoke. Me.

Rushing dust. A truck
Stopped at the petrol pump.
An eye, a ball of meat,
Fixed me in the heat.
Pointed chin. Pointed crown,
Staring at me up and down.
He spat. A bit of German spit.
Then hit my pack and broke the frame.

*   *   *

A diamond man from the USA
Took me to Springbok, all the way.
On we sped ahead of our twin whorls
Of dust and the disc of world came too.

Hills grew on its farthest rim,
Dim and buckling in the heat;
Heaps of dust, boneless dunes
Not unlike the moon's.

Headlamps like an early frost
Were splashing on the dust,
Or patches of the palest yellow
Flowers, primroses of pure light.
Skin and cloth now deeply sallow
On we drove into the night.

*   *   *

The Cape was new, new made almost:
Sea broke in spume along the coast,
Everywhere sea broke clean and white,
Air yellow in the morning light,
Everywhere a quiet boom.

Winter Solstice, 1962

I meet her off the bus.
Already it's midwinter dusk,
The kind of dismal day that tires
And aches. Midland hunting shires,
All hock-deep mud and clay
On this, the shortest day.

A cowl of trees, a hood,
Engulfs us, twin columns
Of deep pain. Mud flows
Like slurry in the lane.

Strings of quiet sleet streak
Across the vale, grey and bleak.
She calls my name and falls,
A memory that still appals.

I drag her on her heels
Under the darkness of a bank,
Clay that feels so cold and dank.

Sleet soaks the greyness
Of her head. That cheap rain
Hood never was much good.

A strain of Victorian pain
Is like a virus in the vein
As she lies dying on the clay
In the darkness of the shortest day.

Navvyman
Then hot summer's here again,
Hill idle in the heat. There's
A vacancy on the garden seat
And none to welcome rain.
Rented soil that once uplifted
An agèd man is green with weed.
Contentment's never guaranteed.

Yet there's still that scent of currant leaves,
That itch of summer after rain,
Rain on rhubarb. Rain on grain.

S.S. *Tapti*
Sun-glint on the sea, and ships,
A lifting early morning mist,
A school of whales that dived and dipped:

On the sea-bed then I found
The wreck of the Tapti, outward bound,
Torpedoed in friendly wartime seas,
Sheltered by the inmost Hebrides.

Her wheel was a floral clock
Of gold and mauve anemones
Swaying in a breeze of tide.
Tock-tock of diesel in the sky.

When the sun at last began to sink
Mull was mauve, then pink,
As evening settled on the isles.

Unscuba'd Sea

You grew quite fond
Of rubbery kelp and fronds
Of bladder wrack and weed
But, scubaman, you can't live there,
An alien with your bottled air.

But what delight it would be
To be alone in an unscuba'd sea
On a blue-hilled planet, people-free.

Sunset West

On the ebb I crossed the bay at Lyme,
But still on passage through the Straits of Time.
Why did I think I'd find my rest
In the sea lanes and the sunset West?
Onedin on the box, I in a boat
On our long south coast:
Nights in ports on little rivers -
Tamar, Dart or Plym,
Or lying low, snug beneath
The wooded hills of Noss Mayo.

Noss Mayo

It's fifty years and more
Since I was there –
Alone and living, now afloat,
Now berthed on ebb-tide sand,
In a small sea-going motor boat,
Young and only half-aware
Of what's beyond the things I saw.

If I could, I would go back in time
To stand on that quay, that riverside,
Sea-fish idling in on a rising tide,
And never waste my passing prime.

Glenelg

Salvation through a place I then sought
In the land of rain and the biting fly,
Over the sea from Skye:

A cottage on the Glenelg plain
By the smithy, the fork in the lane
And the old invader army fort -

All gain, I hoped, and little loss
Under the hills of Wester Ross.

But how misplaced was I
By the cindery Cuillin mountain ridge
In that land of rain and biting midge.

From the Start, 1999

By waysides rich, unbotanised,
(The scent, the sight, was what he prized)
A boy with weightless feet
Was stepping out to meet,
Eternity.

I used to wait for time to pass,
Now the sea and I are wrinkled up:
An alien's in the looking glass,
A man from Sirius Three
Bearded white with shaving foam
And a million million miles from home.

Afterword

How can you live with quiet grace
In this riddle of a people-ridden place,
An alien at ease?

I give you this: Beauty is all we see
At the base of what it is to be.

2. Lichen on a Roof

To divinity we reconnect
Through beauty and the intellect

For beauty is the conductor and the source,
The conduit, channel, cause and course:

Sunlight swayed by shadow
And by shade on pale Palladian walls.

Sensing what the senses cannot see,
All turns on that, the axletree:

All is extra: extra-senses, extra-sense,
Extra-syntax, extra-past-and-future-tense

For we are, as far as I can see,
The living eyes of Eternity.

*   *   *

Beauty too can unveil, disclose,
A mood of sadness and repose

Since sadness somehow always rings
The brevity and loneliness of things:

Sun shaft in woodland gloom,
Sadness in an empty room,

Brevity of shadows on the hill,
Fly buzzing on a window sill,

Sunlight on garden grass,
Things that change, decay and pass.

*   *   *
Stand in a landscape, let its grace
Dissolve you into placelessness-through-place.

Sit in the dunes among marram grass and sand,
Rockless yellow hills trickling through your hand:

Alone in the sifting sand of a summer dune,
There is no sea, no sand, no sound, no summer noon.

*   *   *
Art was once the light that shined
Through beauty and the widened mind

For some can sense divinity, however faint,
Through word or sound or paint.

The stillness in a still-life grape or pear
Is a passage to the great Elsewhere.

Fine pots aren't made of clay
But of ideas from beyond the edge of day.

And listen to the village church clock chime
Breaking through the crust of time:

Cleaving it too is soaring stone
Above the bishop's dishonoured throne:

Hear voices in the cathedral choir
Piercing the lower to meet the higher.

Salvation is also given wing
By the physics of a tautened string

And don't forget that Mozart on a clarinet
Is more than ebony and air.

The beauty that we find in rhyme
Is the same as Beauty outside of time

For we're linked by Plato's iron rings
To the gift the gods alone can bring:

When the gods no longer come,
Mankind lies waste and dumb.

*   *   *

To brief salvation we can be brought
By beauty in ideas and thought:

Ideas that have always stood
Outside of time, like Beauty and the Good:

Abstract rules which govern all,
All ideas too elegant to fail or fall.

They say a theory must be true
If beauty keeps on breaking through:

It's the exoteric that so often comes
Back to Foxe's Book of Martyrdoms.

Watch the webs the spiders spin
To unbar the way to let you in.

*   *   *

In grey rain on an evening hill
There is always something that is still,

Summer stream, summer's day –
To Being, stillness is the common Way

For salvation, I think you'll find,
Comes only to a thought-stopped mind:

We're rowing on a river against the tide
As thought after thought, like oars, are plied

But stop the rowing and then
We and the river are at one again.

We cross in a single stride
The instant thought has died

Though there is no border, no frontier,
No far there and no near here

And so no flash, no crack, no crash,
For we're always there and always here.

* * *

As in a living-room with sliding walls,
On warm summer days, when evening falls,

We barely know when we have passed
From polished floor to garden grass

For the swathing air must make us doubt
Where we are, indoors or out,

So, in the dark (and fathoms deep)
On the very outer edge of sleep

We have a sense of sameness, soul
Stepping from smallness to the Ever-whole:

For in the inner chambers of the mind
An affinity with Infinity we also find

And the doubt-free bed on which we lie
Is the deep sweet Peace of Eternity,

A gift of the gods which only comes
When the bugles cease, and the kettledrums.

*   *   *

Beauty abandoned, we disconnect
The invisible from the intellect.

Beauty embraced will heal the wound
Of being castaway, marooned.

For all of this, I need no proof:
Rain will do, or lichen on a roof.

3. Sea and Seaside

Light the Lamp
An ancient inn sits by a tide
Ebbing in the wood outside:

But no river could ever run
On your dry planet with its saffron sun.

Come then, landlord, light the lamp
Against the evening and the damp.

By the Sea
Sun block cream and hat,
Lilac coffee pot. All that
And sunlight glinting on the sea.

See the ochre sand of summer,
Sea swept,
Sea wet,
Stretching away
By a sand-scarfed bay.

An August sun still smoulders
On waves drooping now like tired shoulders.

Out there's the sparkle of the sea:
Here, fathoms deep, is eternity.

Bournemouth
Glint or glisten?
Listen to the sea's
Soft spill of breath.

Louis d'or or new doubloon
Sparkling in the afternoon,
Each wave's a spill of coin.

Where are the old colonials
Chaired in wickerwork and cane?
You'll never see their likes again.

Out there in the raging west
Is still the great blockade of Brest
And red-haired Drake's in God's Name Bay,
Half a Tudor world away.

Salvation is a sun-glazed
Sea, and all those hazed
And salt-caked days.

Westward
I round Hurst Point
On a milk-pale sea,
Cool but hot-about-to-be.
By compass rose I make a run
In the raging splendour of the sun
Across Lyme Bay
By Portland Bill
On a sea too still
To wet the shingle
On the beach:

Each pebble's graded by the sea,
But not today. No stone scrapes.

Kelp wrack drapes
Eroded rock with straps
Of coagulated sea
As I sail into a sea scent,
A sea light. Port is a rent
In rock still hot from the sun,
And then a Cornish night.

Sunset West II

Once only can you go to where
The rivers of your Eden flow?

Out there in the sunset west
Was where I thought to find my rest
Wearing summer on my face
Steeped in a poetry of place:

Homesick now I guess I am
For the river up at Morwellham
Or dragging anchor in Looe Bay
Waiting for a tide to take me
To the comfort of a riverside.

Wet with river and with rain
King Harry's ferry on her chains
Cranks herself from bank to bank.

St Enodoc

Drink a polystyrene cup of tea
By Padstow and a troubled sea.

Over there is Lyonesse
Where Bedivere took the brand
Excalibur in a knightly hand
For the king, they say, had gone
To the apple isle of Avalon.

Dunes break slow and soft,
Crested like arrested waves,
Upon the bedrock of Bray Hill:
They move yet look so still.

The church of Enodoc,
Is founded not upon a rock
But in a hollow dune.
Lichen, like yellow paint,
Is stippled on a wall. Feel
The nearness of the saint?

God-the-Ghost is rain-wet bark
And evening coming on. And dark.

Cornish Cove

A brook is trickling though
Palms and fleeced bamboo,
Flickering over sand
To a very Cornish sea.

A fishing port of painted stone
Is stacked around its rocky cove.

A pirate man in Cornish rain
Is thinking of the Spanish Main
So many, many ocean miles
West of Tresco and the Cornish Isles.

Fish cellars here once filled with fish
When pilchard was a common dish,
Staining silver the western seas.

Wartime Coastal Road

What flat-nosed Bedford drove
Along this wartime concrete road,
With slitted lights?

A pillbox squats
With ivy-circled
Machine-gun slots.

Look out on 1941
Along the barrel of a gun.

Gaze at 1942
And a river oddly blue.

Rye

From the battlements look down
On an elongated river leaving town
In a blue-mud groove:

Look across to Dungeness
Over the town's unevenness
And rooves so Roman-red.

On the knoll (forget the sea)
Is literature, gentility:
The Jameses here are on the list —
The novel-writer, the Pragmatist —
And the bishop's boy
At the turning of the lane
Before the night the Heinkels came.

Cobbles ripple like a rill
Back through time and down the hill:
Palm-big bricks are russet red,
Monuments to the unnamed dead
In this time unevened town.

French youth go nasalling by.
What brings them all to Rye?
Let them too depart in peace.

The church, not broad perhaps but wide,
Is close against the once-seaside.
The old church clock and its pendulum
Tick you on to Kingdom-Come.
By the Quarterboys a quote
Truly warns that life is brief
But I, who've had enough of grief,
Button up my coat and think of tea.

Soon be summer. What will it add
To the thousand years this town has had?

4. Place

Glenelg Remembered

The lane like a river ran
In that late evening rain.

All day it had rained grey
On a grey sea and the green
Croft meadow. A real river ran
Bent by summer trees.

In gorges, rain leaped,
Heaped into new-made rivers.

Tail lights shone through
Car-made mist
On the river-road
Like river-boat lamps
On a larboard beam.

By the Barrack

Outside is a rage
Of weather and big seas,
Rain from the nearby Hebrides.

Skirt the sheepfold and the pen
In all that streaming nitrogen.
A redcoat once paraded there,
There by the barrack, workhouse-grim:
What, I wonder, became of him?

Sound of Sleight
And then the scent of sea at last
And coffee from the lilac flask
On barnacled and sea-wracked rocks.

Shadows stroke the bulk of Skye:
What else in nature could so caress
That brutal heap of emptiness?

Lying on this headland of the bay
I watch the ferry from Kylerhea
Ply, re-ply, her tide-bent passage
To the Isle of Skye.

Kylerhea
Squint through the narrows
At this summer-sequined sea -

A sea so full of sun a surf
Of light is breaking on a shore
Where that soft sea sucks at sand.

Coral Hills of Cumnor
I.
Of course the coral polyp died
To be reused as a green hillside
Where now a sparrow hops
And pecks on a clovered lawn,
Though gone are reapers in the corn.

Here the fall and rise
Of coral rose to hills
With stones on graves
Too lichened to be read
As slow new life
Obliterates the dead.

On this curve of stone
Against the sky
Is silence, save
For the noise that
Ageing brings:
An old man
Walks on coral
Hills fit for an old
Man's heart
With no steep
Slope that kills.

II.

Walk where Jurassic fish once hid
On hills, not high but coral hard,
With doves and elder and the wheat
Before the coming of high summer heat.

The chime of the church clock bell
On peakless hills in the scent of June
Tells of the coming end of time,
That time is not eternity.

Yet coral will again rise high
Wet with rain against a winter sky
Before this globe rolls round again in ruin.

III.

Sunlight slopes on a sloping sill
To a flagstoned floor where monks
Once knelt, obedient to the passing bell.

Time is ticked by the bell tower clock:
Time is in the silent stillness of the air:
The Timeless too is always here.

In the heat outside I hear
Cavalry canter in Cumnor's lanes:
"Not so", say you, "for time's a string" –
Beads for the Commons, beads for the King.

The Surrey Hills
After the axe, the ox
To plough the Low wet Weald
Today more green and blue
Than that grey and distant sea.
Add these to the things this eye has seen:
Add too weald, wold or wood. All
Wold was wooded, High or Low.

Romania, 1992
Motoring down the Danube plain
Across the river from Ukraine
We find no shade
Save shadows of shadoofs
And wings of storks
Descending on to roofs.

In wintertime the marsh
With ice is brittle, bright and harsh
And Russians in the reeds inbreed.

The filtered Danube flows
Into a sea where a bireme plies
With painted sail and painted eyes.
An emperor fought barbarity
Down here. Ovid wrote of change.

Moontide
How big would a moontide be
If the moon had mountains in a sea?
Tides a hundred furlongs high
Bringing dinner to barnacles in the sky
While the big blue globe of earth
Is rising on the raging near horizon?

No arid yellow, but a watery green,
And who would call Selene then serene?

Sunset on Titan and Europa

What, I wonder, would it be like to walk
Alone on those methane hills
Above the methane seas of Titan?

Or stand alone on that cold
Ice moon, cracked and floed,
A land-less, hill-less world
Of curving ice encasing
A moon-sized ball of water?

To be alone on the outer rim,
The setting sun so distant, dark and dim?

Photograph, Burma, 1944

A lean lance-jack, a milkman-
Muleteer, smiles in youth
Across the years. Ladling milk
From door to door, he'd never
Heard of the Service Corps.

Out of Burma did he ever come?
Outlive the old Millennium?

The long battalions march away
From Rangoon and Mandalay.

Autumn Evening, Northants

Rain and air are grey as day dies
In a rain-dark dusk-green end of day.

Remember the scent
Of hinted at decay
In ochre-coloured late October?

November was grey with mist,
A caw of rooks, voles in silty brooks
Sluggish by spinneys in shoe-clogging clay
Under undulating ironstone hills.

Late Night Café
October comes with daylong rain
As in the failing evening light I drink
Coffee in the bright café:

Of rain from off the western sea I think,
Of Rooke who broke the boom in Vigo Bay.

The young today are taught to mock
Cloudesley Shovell who took the Rock?

And what today are the young to make
Of Admiral Benbow or of Blake?

Blake sailed his fleet beneath the black
Volcanic peak, all pale with snow:

Silver galleons rode below
The Spaniard's guns, afraid to go

Yet still within Blake's daring reach:
He took them by the black-sand beach.

For taking gold from Tenerife
Blake, I take it, is now a thief?

Paternoster Square
It's evening and the shortest day.
The City's shut and half the town
Is closed. Tomorrow's day-lit
Day will be longer than today's
Because yesterday and tomorrow
Are the second shortest days

For there are pyramids
Of longer and lessening light
Diamond-shaping down the years.

What waits ahead out there
Beyond the diamond's widest point?

Summer came late. In August, I went
In sunshine through the fields of Kent.

August Hamlet, Kent,
This old hamlet and its unstraight street
Is abandoned to high summer heat:
Sun shines on thatch and stone.

In the silence of August a man
And his summer stand hatless alone.

Kent Country Church
What can a talking cassock say
That silence in the nave
Has left unsaid? Why tell
Us what is meant
When silence is a sacrament
And outside is a canopy of summer?

Cumnor and Canterbury
The shadow of a mullion,
Sharp and still, lies
On a medieval window sill
And eternity is camera-caught.

On a dry, dry-summer lawn
Shadows of the cloisters also lie –
All summers past caught in a square
Of camera-isolated grass.

5. Bollards

Woden
Summer never seemed to shine
So a priest has broken Woden's shrine.

From *bletsian* to bless,
From bled and bleed to bliss?
Where is Beauty in all of this?

Back Through Time
Prowling over Primrose Hill
A sabre'd tiger caught and killed
A rhino by the palms that grew
Where stand the cages now of London Zoo:
Before, that is, the bear bore down
To feed on berries in Camden Town.

Greenness fills the air and eyes
As you climb that hill for exercise:

Towers not to scrape a sky
But gouge, to scratch, to graze
An eye. Like it if you can,
Brain-abrading Barbican.

Protected by Romana Pax
Hob-nailed Roman sandal'd feet
Walked from the Walbrook to the Fleet
Long before St Mary Axe,
Yet all are grave-gripped now.

Saxon Botolph, Celtic Bride,
Comely by a riverside.

So little cheer, so much gloom,
Depression in so large a room:
An altar, like an empty stall,
Is void of any goods at all.

Yet men rode stone upon the sea
To convert the wild Cornovii,
People of an almost-isle.

Petroc sailed a grinding stone
(No need of ballast to keep her trim),
God, I guess, accompanied him.

One man rowed a cabbage leaf.
I'd pay to own a bit of his belief.

Alien Afternoon

On a long Victorian street –
Like a flue conveying heat –
High-stooled within a coffee shop
Fan-cooled, but hot,
Stirring coffee with a coffee spoon
On an alien summer afternoon
I note in every wayward face
How undivine's the human race.

Human shoals respond
And shift like mackerel in a tide.
(Don't mind me, I lack the bond
To bind me to mankind,
In fact can barely comprehend
The meaning of a friend.)

The tarmac underneath my feet
Is plasticining in the heat,
Sol-softened for soft-soled men:
Beware that blazing carcinogen.

On Primrose Hill bipeds prowl
And mate where once a tiger growled
And ate a woolly rhino by the Zoo.

Mankind is milling here in droves:
Did God-the-Logos really cook
Their carbon in his cosmic stoves?

St Pancras Workhouse
Here's the workhouse, grimed and grim.
Who could ever worship Him?

Crimson tunic'd they would sit
Jailed in blackened yellow brick
While early morning men in hobnail boots
Were blackened by the coal yard chutes.

The all-night locos they could hear,
Slow, with boilers fed, toiling from
The engine shed. And in the rain
And in the shine, wagons rolling
Down the line by that place of pure
Despair. Coal from collier to smoke in air.

Here's the chapel where they'd prate
Of hope. A ha'p'ny rate it must have meant
To build to poverty a monument so great.

The Incompletes
Ecclesiastic prisons fill
With men the bishop plans to kill.

For reading English'd Holy Writ
Little Bilney's burned alive
At Norwich in the Lollard's Pit.

The cloaca's in full spate
In Thomas More. He's far
From catholic in his hate.

*   *   *

"Be true hearted unto God,"
Says Tyndale in his Tudor way.
"Faith will save you all one day."

A scaled-down Satan said to Eve:
"Tush, ye shall not die." She'd
Caught the Devil in the world's first lie.

*   *   *

Horses stamp their iron-shod hooves,
Casting divots with their shining shoes.
The cavalry of God. All that discipline
To chastise sin.

Reason, they say, is passion's slave,
So glass is shivered in the nave.

And all the while the horses' hooves
Break up the turf as if to prove
No man – no God – can now resist
The fury of the fundamentalist.

*   *   *

Soot-black drizzle. Grime.
And then the clocks begin to chime
In a parlour overstuffed.
Dust. Monotony and must.

Better be on Saturn's moons
Than endure those dusty
Sunday afternoons.

All Saints, Margaret Street
In pigmented light and painted gloom
God's present in a pointed room
Where manger and the magi meet on tile?

Crimson saints are here, and saffron, too,
While the chapel is all gilt and gold.
Above, the steeple bell is tolled.

Soprano notes and granite arches
Are soaring to a painted roof.
Can this place be devil-proof?

In rising smoke, an incense haze,
The cry is all for mercy and for praise
And Thomas Cranmer's guilt and fear.

Small men made big by cope or cape
Proclaim the living God is dead
Then serve Him up alive in bread.

Gargoyle
The Cathedral Close, and midnight chimed
A dozen cracked uncertain times
On a cold midwinter solstice night
With yellow frost on cobblestones
And pallid sodium light.

"There's the bishop," Gargoyle cried.
"Bishop, beneath your fish's head,
Don't you think that Christ is dead?

You princes of the English church
Have left poor sinners in the lurch."

Then the disbelieving Gargoyle said:
"God's in the ferry in the rain
But absent where the jack-boots stamp
Inside the concentration camp?"

Quakerman (1633–1694)
Coxery, linguister to his mates,
Was lading herring for the Straits.
Lion's Whelp or Sparrow Pink,
To become a Quaker, don't you think,
Is a folly on which you'll sink?

Like flukes of air, catastrophe
Beats upon a user of the sea
But a Quakerman can't doff a hat
To painted saint or, come to that,
Fire a gun yet in the Trade
A man is paid to kill,
Think of killing what you will.

But Coxery is in love's soft grip,
God-taken from a meaner fellowship.

*   *   *

Avalon or Apple Isle
That mind holds matter, like hills in mist,
Is the insight of the immaterialist:

But if this be true, and Mind is King,
Then the grave's a gate to greater things?

In death perhaps we still can keep
The peace we meet in age's me-less sleep?

Beyond this life, Mind may let you smile
In an Avalon, or Apple Isle?

Hills and headlands stretch away
From Plymouth Sound and Deadman's Bay.

6. Antiquity

Ulysses
Cyclops tall as trees
Circle the bay, baying,
Baleful. Baneful.
Leave them all behind,
The monocular and the blind.

But, then, hove-to
By cove and cave,
From a god you go
To strive and bicker
By a portico
Though all want to lie
Circe'd in ease,
Unable to die.

The Odyssey in Brief
Why leave a morning world
For a world of mourning:
Immortal life for war
And mortal wife and dung
And dying dogs on a rock
Too short for horses?

Penelope
Nausicaa came with mules
And easy wheels
By slow up-welling pools
Yet Penelope's pull is stronger.

What is it that blind Homer sees
In this tale of striving Ulysses,
That love-driven man
Who strove for home?

Sappho by Moonlight

Sappho loved a world of whiteness,
Of moonlight white on Lydia
And on the sea, blanching
The white leaved woods of Lesbos.

But Sappho also loved the risen sun
And Aphrodite rising from the sea.

Apollo Ignored

Apollo's dictum still applies –
Know Thyself:
But who now tries
In these late days, lost
To continuity and time?

What does the great Apollo say?
"Let ego go to let you be
Ego-free in Arcady"?
Et in Arcadia Ego was said by Death
Yet since the eternal mind is bliss
There is in Arcady no Dis.

Aegean Blue

For Plotinus, colour
Was the simplest route
To Being, or the Absolute.

What blue seas,
I wonder, did Plato meet
Between Syracuse and Crete?

Sophocles

"Not to be is best," said Sophocles
And countless billions have been unborn.

Do the unborn need the aid
Of sunlight idle on a wall
To pierce the mud of what is made
To what's eternal without change?
To be is surely what is strange.

To the Cape: Three Anchor Bay
I went looking for a room
In a rooming house all dark
Inside; clinker built, an ark
With a shaky belvedere.
A woman, kit-bag-bra'd,
In badly faded purple fard,
Kept watch upon the gangplank there
With promised joys. "I wanna nice
Clean boys." Each room was purple too:
Drapes and bed and purple mat
On lino fading then to blue.
"Six poun' I wanna for dat
Room. One hour, two hour,
You come back?"

But there you never did unpack.
What sowing of wild oats
Did you then miss? Instead you went
To stay by crayfish boats and palm
Trees by a bay.

*   *   *

"I've ruined you," with spite she said.
The waiter sidled back to serve
Steak-in-toast. "You boast
About me, don't you? To your friend?"

Gingham like a frock
Covered tabletop and pane.
The lady ate again,
Sucking cattle grease
From knuckle to the nail.

"I have to marry. Don't you see?"
(Thank God, I think, it wasn't me.)
"David's rich but wants to touch."
(I thought of crayfish boats
Above the beach.) I said:
"I guess in time he'll want his oats."

"You're a thing without a spine"
(And I too thought so at the time).

Fumblingly I paid. Afraid
And flustered, I left too much,
Lacking a common or a kingly touch.

"You left a tip?" "Half a crown."
"You little rubbish, get it back."

Later I wrote it down,
That tale of Juddering Jack
In the oddness of that town.
"Sixpence only you should have left."
Of such small change was life then made,
And palm trees on an Esplanade.
"Where has she gone," I wonder now,
"With wizened skin and wrinkled brow?"

Durban Bay
An un-macho Hemingway
Is beached in Durban Bay:
His shadow in the sea
Floats below the clash
Of sun and iron-filing fish.

"I'm on the rocks."
"Where did you hear
That I take bribes?"
"Around the docks."
Angrily he cries:
"Who told you this?"
"I have no friend."
A salt sea hissed outside.

Strip a label with a fingernail:
Pour gas and cold and beer
Into that seething wilderness of fear,
Foot juddering on a rail
In a brandy scented,
Liner shaded, bar.

Ink and Think, 1982,
She introduced us – Camera,
Sound, Director with his paunch.
"And this," she said at last of me,
"Is Ink and Think." We all smiled
As we all stood by that lake in Galloway,
Its white sand beach, unpeopled hills.

Where is she now, I wonder,
That young PA, old if still
Alive, with her wit of Ink
And Think in Galloway's
Lowland hills? Perhaps she
Too now knows that youth
And thought don't always mix:

Some need age in which to think –
In youth they merely learn to use the ink.

Swillicking Dick, 1885
Haymaking time, '85,
Swillicking Dick is on the loose
Contemplating how to mooch
A drum of tea, a shive of bread.

In a rutted lane at dusk
White idling smoke he notes.
Rattle of sneck,
Creak of heck:

"Yah bain't ourn!"
Pertly she stares
At the loafer leaning there.

"Dab o' butter? Rib o' beef?
To give a navvy some relief?"

"Who bist thee? Thee bist big!"

"Needful, missus, for to dig
With shovel and with pick."

"Ourn's a carter, gone to town.
Beef ortins? Do sit down."

He takes a clasp knife for a fork.
"Tha's nobbut a bairn to be a wife."

"Where shall yah sleep?" (Growing bold.)

"Under a hedge."

"That shall be cold."

"Happen."

"Better afore a fire."

"Better in a feather bed."

Not long wed, she blushes pink.
"Pity though I ain't got one."
Her bodice is undone.
"A bolster I can lay atween.
No harm in that." He is keen,
Prising off both boots and hat.

Trail:
1. Tolmers Square
"All right? Okay? All right?"
Stammers duffle-coated Jack
(The date is still pre-anorak).

"You're right. Shocking cold."
Already she is very old.

"No, Christmas ain't the same.
All the costers used to sing,
Especially after Mafeking."

By gaslight I note it down
Under the hill in Camden Town.
"Weren't the old days bad?"

"A little pony and a trap
For crabs my Granfer had."

"The old days? Weren't they bad?"

"Yes. Them was good old days.
Them winkles come in trays
From the eel shop oppo-sight.
Good old days. You're right.

My Granny used to send me round
Selling walnuts up in Camden Town.
The old Goat public, to workmen there."

We're pooled in yellow light.
"If the crop was good they'd pay
A shilling a bushel for them hops.
What's he say?"

"It's not the same."

"Who's to blame?"

"It's changed."

"He's right. I say you're right."

I'm aching on a hardwood chair
In a lino'd room in Tolmers Square,
Fugitive from the old Queen's reign,
Times that never now can come again.

"Pease pudding you could get,
And saveloys." Outside is wet.
"Many of them pies I've ate.
Penny pies from Sweeney Todd,
Him as had the barber shop."

Jack the Ripper, Juddering Jack,
Them days won't never now come back.

II. Bigbury Bay

Sea-valley and green hillside,
Smelling of river and of tide:
Across the harbour bar
The whole far
World peeled open wide
Into a western sky

Of paint and clarity:
She, a column of content,
I, in torment
By her side.

Below our keel, I knew,
Were wide-eyed wrasse, and weed
Blowing in a tide.
With the Mewstone on the bow,
A breeze began to rise
And I began to doubt
But was, I realise,
Too afraid of fear to put about.

Waves heaped high above our heads.
Seas like hills swooped by:
We were, we knew, about to die.
"Sorry. Sorry," was all I said.

"Poor boy." A hand touched mine.
I'd met the human-and-divine.

III. Evening

Another Autumn Sunday evening settles in,
Stripping summer from the bough,
And we've survived another day, somehow.

"That's right," she says, "I only had two
Hats. A red one and a blue. And whatever
Happened to that cat, I'd like to know?
But what can a poor girl do?"

"Golden dust I suppose you think
You've got. Poor little beggar. See how
The fish wound up? Such a row!"

Pre-dusk light has given out and a day-long
Gale is ending. A church clock chimes,
Across the roof tops, eight cracked times.

"You'd like some tea perhaps?"

"Unseal your maps. I'm having tea
Tomorrow with the Queen."

"What do you mean?"

"She wants to chit."

"You mean to chat?"

"In the chapel."

"But dressed like that?"

"A quote of God. I hear it all.
Such a pity what happened to St Paul."

Cameret
In Gib they're drinking
Blackstrap wine to Lord St Vincent
And St Valentine. But Capperbar
Can't run away from the rocks
Of Camaret. God help us,
God-the-Ghost, upon this Savage
Coast. Rain is raining bright within
The taffrail's yellow lantern light.

Capperbar in sennit hat
Is the antithesis of Jolly Jack.

The pigtailed timoneer
Biting on his quid
Has never had to rid
Himself of fear.

The quartermaster scans the leech,
The long horizon and the skies:
He never looks behind the eyes.

How can they live so unafraid
Of a chain-shot loaded carronade?

Here's a savagery
Not alone of stone
And spray: Hawke
And Howe are in the bay.

Hogged and broken on the shore
Or all a-wallow in a surf
That will not serve
To ride a ship, are men o' war.

Capperbar

Niobe now is sailing large,
Headed for the great blockade.
Capperbar sits slewed, afraid.
Gundeck's raining, reeking, dim:
What of comfort can we say to him?

No contentment's here. No woman's thighs.
It's better when desire dies.
All winter long we'll see no sun
And the war has twenty years to run.

Bare poles wag leafless against the sky.
"Out or down, lads. Out or down.
You're a long way now from Plymouth town."

"Our ships have ringed the western sea
And closed the coast of Brittany."

Long Atlantic rollers sweep,
Depriving men of rest or sleep,
Bursting in the Roads of Brest.

We're in bewitchment's grip.
Eight bells. The long night watch
Begins. Feel the long Atlantic fetch
Lift and pitch each groaning ship.

Stinking burgoo, butter's rancid lumps,
Nightlong labour at the pumps.

We have braces now to splice
In driven salt that flays
The skin, and spray
Like splintered ice.

Prowling corporals creep and probe. "Dowse
That glim." Snow is warmer than the rain
That frees the rigging once again.
"Do you hear there, sleepers? Rouse."

In your hammock hear
The ship's skin creak:
Seams gape open wide and leak
And you are man-shaped fear.

* * *

We're standing into Plymouth Sound
From Penlee Point to Cawsand Bay.
"Bumboats, sir, and women on their way."
Soon they're swarming all around.

Rum or ale's for sale, and women too.
Now, Capperbar, what will you do?
Let me tell you this once more,
You cannot even step ashore
Because the Navy tells you so:

Accept with grace this little lull
For encapsulated in this hull
Is a certainty you cannot flout
For all your philosophy of doubt.

"Who goes there?" the guffy shouts:
The smack of a half-spent musket shot
Is sure to make your shoulder blade grow hot.

*   *   *

The bosun's mate takes up the whip
As a silence settles in the ship.

Pain is everywhere: in eyes, in hair,
Everywhere but in your back.

The second stroke will break the skin,
The open wound of discipline.
Your back is ridged for life.

*   *   *

The Captain's pig-and-chicken farm
Is by the Sick Bay in the bow
Where Capperbar lies broken now
With only vinegar for balm.

Mr Price, a doctor in a periwig,
Wipes brandy from his lips:
Veteran of a dozen ships,
He's oblivious of the squealing pig.

"Good case of ship fever over there.
Burning up with petechiae."
He fixes his only eye on Capperbar.
"The loblolly boy will wash his feet
To dissipate the heat
But he very soon will die...
You there, idlers! Stow that din!"

His patient's messmates tumble in:
Old Daddy, tall Yankee Bray,
Young Davy, small Benny May.

Yankee grips a leather can.
"You'll take a swig?"
The pig is squealing for its swill.
"You took your flogging like a man."

They've all been drinking hard.
"Purser's swipes it ain't."
Pure brandy then, with just a taint
Of tar. "Smuggled in a ball of lard."

*   *   *

"Masthead! Where away?"
"Larboard beam. Across the bay."
"Get an offing. Wear the ship.
Tonight there'll be a little trip."

"Sway out the boats." They clear the booms
Encased in blackness like a grave,
And then the ancient softness of the wave.
Over them *Niobe* looms.

Midnight-black. No moon. Black
Ship is hidden by black sea and sky.
Many a man is going to die
Before the boats are safely back.

Yet what a pleasant place to be, steeped
In night and an ancient scent of sea.

A following sea, an easy ride,
And then the loom of the frigate's side
And a broadside's roaring overhead.

Red cutter reaches the starboard bow:
Adrenalin will disallow
All fear. Follow the Gunner, Mr Cash,
Over the cathead to cut and slash,
Lit by no lantern but the flash

Of guns. With boarding pike
Young Davy stuns and kills, godlike
Unaware of death. Yankee strikes
With every breath. Gunfire shines,
Staining hull and rigging red,
Blazing on the newly dead.
Human tubing hangs like vines.

Capperbar, you're head to head
With a red-haired Celt from Brittany:
Pull a pistol from your belt
And shoot him dead.

It's darker now. Battle's done:
The gunners all are dead. Gone
With them is the fire that shone
In a blaze of gunlight like the sun.

*   *   *

Here's the Purser, Mr Jones:
The belly in his lap
Is hanging from a thick fat-strap.
I don't believe he's built on bones:

He's growing fatter every day
On food he's paid to give away.

Make chowder in your iron pot:
Fatty pork
And share of shark
And dough with water from the scuttlebutt.

Peg-leg Bandy is the Cook.
"Stew this, sir?" "What's that you say?"
"One tot, sir? Payable Saturday?"
He stows it in his stove with one black look.

Chowder's good. Cheese is rank:
No wonder the Purser's office stank.

The talk now turns to other things to eat:
"Soft tommy and sausage."
"Murphies and cabbage."
"Bacon. Egg."
"Leg of lamb."
"Ham!"
But not off Brest in the vanguard of the fleet.

"Shark," Old Daddy say, "he can't eat me,"
Showing tattooed crosses on arm and knee.
"The cross he works just like a charm"
(Such is the wisdom of the sea).

"I've seen crabs devouring men,"
Says Yankee Jack. "Jamaica, '94.
By the Palisades along the shore.
It was yellow fever time back then."

"Inches deep we buried them
And crabs just dug them up again.
Dug them from their shallow graves."

"What causes it?" asks Capperbar.
"The reek of vegetation in the night."
 "Nothing cures it?" "No, that's right."
Creak of ship and reek of men and tar.

"It did for us, that yellow jack."
"We lay too close to land."
"Skin as yellow as the sand
We laid them in." "Your sick is black."

Young Davy says: "That yellow jack!
Only fifty of us left
That isle." He looks bereft.
"The Gunner brought us back."

Time to sit and think.
"What's in lemon and in lime
That cures the scurvy every time?"
Grog time, now. Time to sit and drink.

*   *   *

Then to Plymouth once again
To take in stores and quotamen.

One's a Cockney, Henry Blair,
All bare tendons, lean and quick,
Whippy as a withy stick
Or high-strung whippet with a hare.

"As a follower of Paine
You'll have everything to gain.

Freight balloons will fill the air
Along with ships that steam and glide
Into the wind. They're on the Clyde
Right now. We're almost there.

Think how things will surely be
When this old world's in smithereens -
Fat mechanics floating in machines
And no poor sailormen at sea.

Think about *this*, then:
Work half a day
For a full week's pay
And live like gentlemen.

All these things can surely be
With just a little mutiny."

*   *   *

Flynn is sailing by another chart,
Swearing-in young Irishmen
With a cross above the heart.

"The King of England, Mr Guelph,
Is as mad as any addled dub
While Florizel, his elder cub,
Thinks only of himself.

Who can then explain to me
Why they're the rulers of my country?"

*   *   *

In a dotted line of shade and sun
Men with neckerchiefs above their ears
Are standing to each gun:
Eighteen pounders, buff and grey,
Each sharply lit by one square ray:
Sea-light speckles the deckhead beams
And *Niobe's* creaking in her seams.
Listen to the ripple of the sea.

See the Frenchman's billowing sail
And her tar-black martingale
Sharp against the glisten of the sun.
"Fire at will." Put linstock to the quill.

Let go the tacklefalls:
Sponge, cartridge, wad and ball.

Trucks grumble up against the sill,
Smoke coils, pink with flame,
Stopping us from taking aim.

Wad and ram, ram and ball,
Tail on the tacklefalls and haul.

Lilac gun smoke's on the sea.
"Alive, are we?" "What?" "Hurt?"
"Alive, I think. Just caked in dirt."
Young Davy's lost his knee.

"You there, idlers, on your feet.
Sweep away the shambles and the reek,
Disregard the shrieks of men."
Pigs root for human meat.

Young Davy's on the orlop, dim
And dark. He doesn't beg:
By candlelight light he'll lose his leg.
What of comfort can we say to him?

*   *   *

Rain is falling through a kinder night.
It's three o'clock, or seven bells.
Lookouts call that all is well.
South we're heading now for Spain.

Powder splutters. There's a shot.
In the flash we see the face of Flynn,
That misbegotten Jacobin.
His rebellion has begun:
He's killed the sentinel
With a small handgun.

Bayonets briefly glisten red.
The Captain at his cabin door
Is calm amid the ship's uproar.
Three more mutineers are dead.

Flynn quickly now turns cat-in-pan
And grips poor Capperbar. "Your man,
Sir, here's your man. He fired the shot
That killed the sentry on the spot."

*   *   *

Capperbar, there's nothing you can do.
The fleet's hove-to outside Cadiz:
Court-martial time it is for you:
After the mutiny at Spithead
They need a body lying dead
And it doesn't matter who.

"Did this book inspire your plan?"
"Sir, it is not mine."
The Captain has been lavish with the wine.
"It's called *The Rights of Man*
And was found within your kit.
You must surely know of it?"

"I'm a printer, sir, from near Liskeard."
We hear a snort
(The Admiral is suffused with port).
"You're a seaman in the afterguard."

*   *   *

A rising sun, a Cyclops eye,
Will watch you as you die.

Boats set out from all the ships.
In each a gun
Is glinting in the sun.
Niobe curtsies low, and dips.

Capperbar, now glory in each sense,
Feel *Niobe* lift and heave,
Sense it all before you leave,
Your last experience:

Note how ochre are the hills,
How deeply yellow is the sun,
How glinting is the long sea-run.

Your neck will never break. You'll choke
As they hoist you like a flag
Through the death-gun's yellow smoke.

Sun and dust and heat
Are rising over Spain.
Boats scatter through the fleet.

8. Hills of Age

Life has gone. There was no plan
But now I've paid the ferryman.